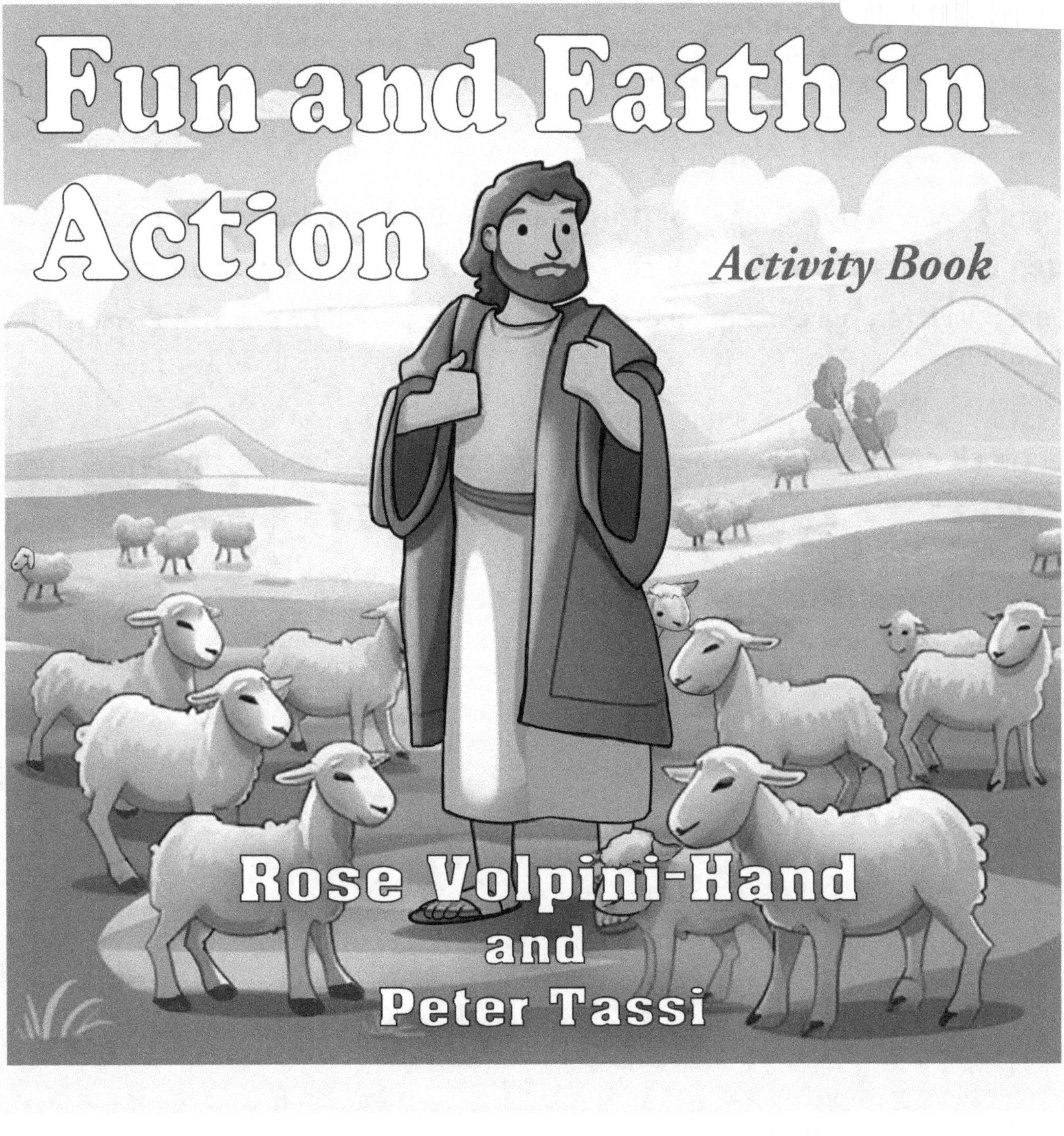

Fun and Faith in Action

Activity Book

Rose Volpini-Hand
and
Peter Tassi

Think of some of the people who care about you. Tell how they help you.

_____

_____

_____

_____

_____

_____

_____

_____

Below make a picture of your teacher helping you.

BECOMING A FORGIVING PERSON

Sin is when we do things that cause us to break relationships with the ones we love.
We sin when we hurt or destroy something that is good.

In the 4 areas of your life, tell how you can improve your relationship.

GOD	SELF	OTHERS	NATURE

An Invitation to My Party!

Make an invitation inviting some friends to your party. This is a party where you can get to know your friends better. It will be a special celebration.

Tell your friends what they will be doing when they come to your party.

Everyone has something special to give us.

We can learn how special each person is, by sharing our time with each one of them

FILL IN THE BLANKS

happy
cross
died
help
pray
heaven
God
Mary
love
life

1. Jesus was afraid, so He went into the garden to _____.
2. Jesus asked his Father for _____.
3. Jesus knew that he had to do what his_____ asked.
4. Jesus knew that one day He would be with his Father in _____.
5. Jesus knew he would be _____ with his Father in heaven.
6. Jesus_____ on the cross for you and me.

Heaven is a wonderful place where God will love and take care of us forever.

Make a picture of what you think Heaven is like. Put 5 things in your picture of what you want to be with you in Heaven.

UNSCRAMBLE THE WORD
AND ANSWER THE QUESTIONS

1. It is lit during Mass, and makes the church bright.

delcans

_____

2. It is on the alter, and reminds us of Jesus' love.

scros

_____

3. Father gives us this to remember God's love and have in us.

drbea

_____

4. This person says Mass.

tpsrei

_____

5. This is when we bring up our Gifts.

fofteyr

_____

6. We sing this in church.

gnso

_____

Make up 3 words for the class to Unscramble.

2 _____   3 _____

Whenever we argue or fight with someone, it is like a storm in our lives. For each storm we must create a a rainbow of Peace.

Write down 5 words that describe a stormy time, and 5 words that describe Peace.

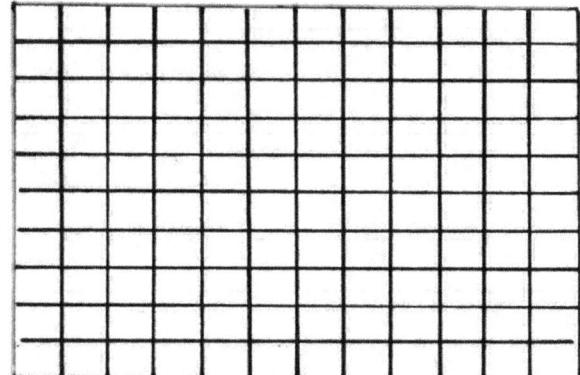

In each circle draw a weapon of war, e.g; rifle bomb tank, etc.

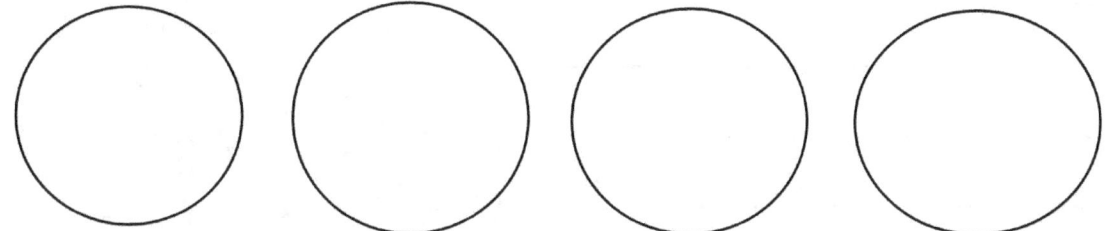

To change the weapons into something Peaceful, write a short poem for each picture.

1._____

2._____

3._____

4._____

WRITE A NOTE TO JESUS

thanking Him for all the gifts He has given You!

_____

_____

_____

_____

_____

_____

_____

_____

_____

_____

_____

_____

_____

Thank you!

YOU ARE BEING CHALLENGED TO GROW!

You are being asked to become a better person.

Use this tree to judge how you are growing. Cut out as many leaves as you need, color them red and yellow.

Red leaves: Write talents, gifts and qualities you have.

Yellow leaves: Write talents, gifts and qualities you are trying to develop.

AN ACROSTIC FOR EASTER

An acrostic poem uses each letter in a word to start a line in a poem.

Ex: **C**ute and Yellow.
Happy tweeting
Inside, outside
Coming to play
Keeping safe by Mommy

Make up your own poem using an Easter word.

_____
_____
_____
_____
_____
_____
_____
_____
_____
_____
_____

Think of someone on TV asking questions. We learn about people by asking good questions.

Write 5 questions that you would ask these people. Ask a friend to play a part of one of these people, and answer your questions.

_____
_____
_____
_____
_____
_____
_____
_____
_____
_____

Jesus, Mary, Soldier, Peter

When Jesus rose from the dead, the Apostles were very excited and happy. They were no longer afraid.

He has risen!

Answer the questions:

1. Why did the Apostles stop being afraid?

_____
_____
_____

2. How does Jesus take away your fears?

_____
_____
_____

Do This Puzzle

Use the letters in the word Resurrection and make 5 words that tell how you feel.

R
E STRONG
S
U
R
R
NICE
C
T
I
O
NEW

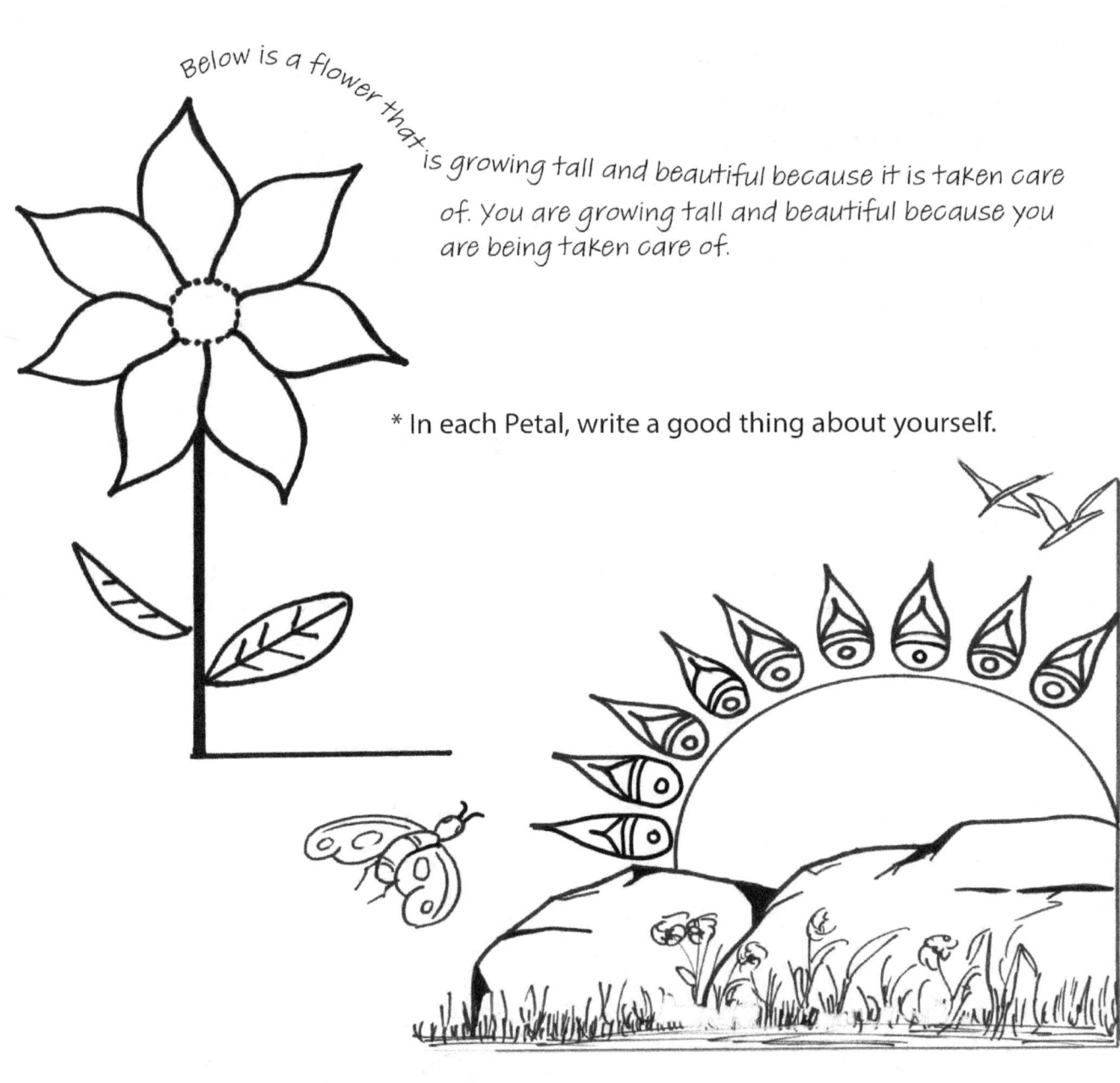

Below is a flower that is growing tall and beautiful because it is taken care of. You are growing tall and beautiful because you are being taken care of.

* In each Petal, write a good thing about yourself.

I AM SPECIAL TO GOD

Jesus call each of us to do a special job on earth.
Everyone has a special gift that helps us do our job

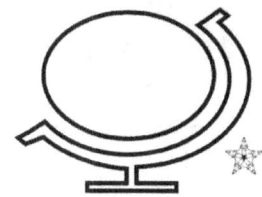

Here is a list of people who have jobs to do. Tell what their jobs are.

Parents _____

_____

Teacher _____

_____

Priest _____

_____

Bishop _____

_____

Altar Server _____

_____

Custodian _____

_____

WE ARE A *loving* COMMUNITY

YOU ARE SPECIAL
and you have something
to offer others.

Tell 5 nice things about   yourself that you want
others to know. Colour the   heart, cut it out, and display it.

WHAT A PLACE!

Sometimes we go to special places where we meet people we like, and experience God's gifts and treasures with nature.
The Earth is filled with God's great love for us.

Draw a picture of a place that you have visited and experienced God's gifts and treasures.

SAME / DIFFERENT

Would it be a better world if everyone was the same? _____
If not why do we always try to be like others? _____
_____
_____
_____
_____
_____

In the chart below, show how TV and friends influence our decisions and choices.

What do you think Jesus and his friends are saying as they share holy bread?

COLOUR THE PICTURE

When you have a party, you cut a cake and give a piece to each of your friends. Sometimes your Mom puts ice cream on the cake to make it more special. When your friends eat the cake they remember you and celebrate the special time together.

When Jesus called all of his friends together to celebrate a very special time, they shared Holy Bread with Jesus.

Jesus told his friends that after he died they would have the Holy Bread to remind them of Him. Today when we take the Holy Bread, it reminds us that Jesus is with us. He helps us to be good and do the right thing.

*On a seperate piece of paper, make a picture of your birthday party.

Jesus shares Holy Bread with his friends

A Poem by St.Francis of Assisi

Eternal Father
invisible and far away
I owe you my silence and my song
For you are God and everything
belongs to you

Good is your hand that made all things that
are good is brother sun
who offers us another day who bursts
with beauty and shining power
Who blinds and overwhelms us consoles
and makes us glad and gives us life

Good is sister moon,
so pretty with her stars which you have
spun from heaven:
and good like you is brother wind with
all his blowing clouds and weather good
and bad and air in which we live

CELEBRATING

NATURE

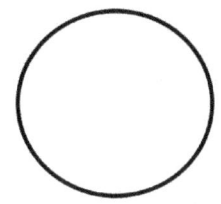

We go to church to share in our love for Jesus
and to be with friends.

Tell why you like going to Church.

FILL IN THE BLANKS

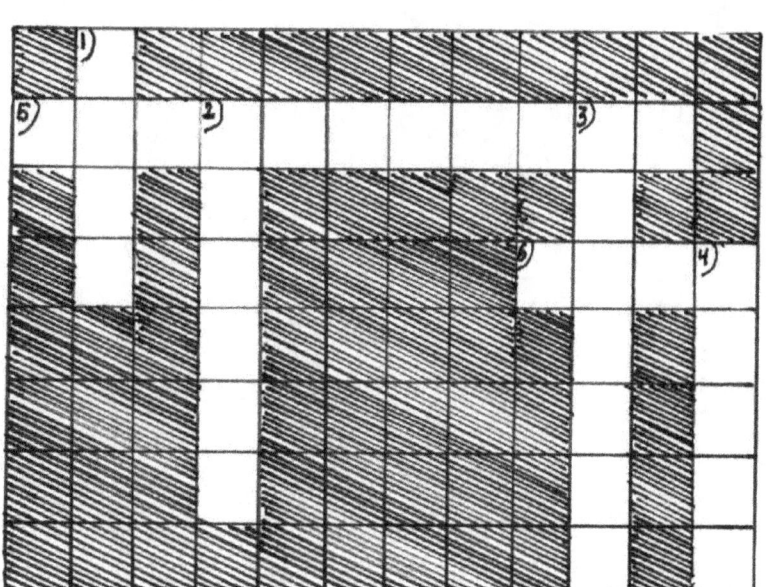

Down

1. Jesus said, "I _____ you."
2. Jesus shared and was very _____.
3. Jesus says you are _____.
4. We should live in _____.

Across

5. When we forgive someone it is called _____.
6. Never be afraid to ask Jesus for _____.

HURTING WORDS

what are some of the things we say to others that can hurt them?

Words are powerful. They can HURT or HEAL!

what are some of the things we say that can heal them?

PARADOX

A paradox is something that sounds absurd but is true.
One paradox is that the more laws we have, the more freedoms we enjoy.
Eg; Thou shalt not kill... this gives us the freedom to walk the streets safely.

Make a list of laws you have at home, at school, and your city. Tell which freedom goes with each law.

_____
_____
_____
_____
_____
_____
_____
_____
_____
_____
_____
_____
_____
_____
_____
_____
_____
_____
_____

JESUS' laws

When we read some of Jesus' teachings we understand that he wants us to obey laws that gives us freedom. (You've already listed some of those laws).
Jesus gave us the 8 Beatitudes to help us be more free.

Read the Beatitudes to help us be more free.

BEATITUDE	FREEDOM
1. Gives of themselves to help others	
2. Prays for others.	
3. Is humble.	
4. Does what God asks.	
5. Shows mercy to others.	
6. Does good deads.	
7. Works for Peace.	
8. True to themselves.	

FAVOURITES

There is always a special person in your life that teaches you a lot, takes you to special places, and gives you lots of gifts. Sometimes that person is a close relative, or friend.

Show that person you appreciate everything she or he has done.
Design a "thank you" card to give to that person.

INCARNATION

Jesus came to earth to give us the knowledge, and the strength, and the faith, to break down barriers.

God becoming human is called the

INCARNATION

Use the word "incarnation," to list some of the gifts Jesus brought us.

INCARNATION

f
i
e
n
d
s
h
i
p

When you are finished, box in the puzzle and make a crossword puzzle from it. Only use the words you need.

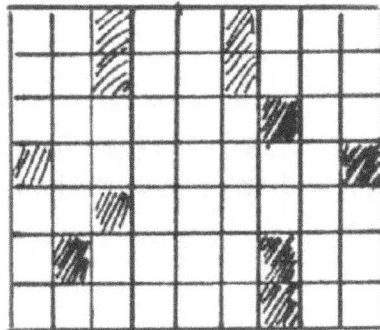

YOU'RE OKAY

Choose a partner.
Each of you decide to write a paragraph about the other.
Write about the good qualities you see in your partner.
When you have finished writing about your partner, give it to him/her.

Dear_____,
I think about you _____
_____
_____
_____
_____
_____
_____
_____
_____
_____

CELEBRATE FRIENDS

Draw a heart for each student in your class.
Write the students name around the heart.
Inside the heart, write one talent or gift that you see in that person.

Example:
JAMES
You are honest

OUR LAND

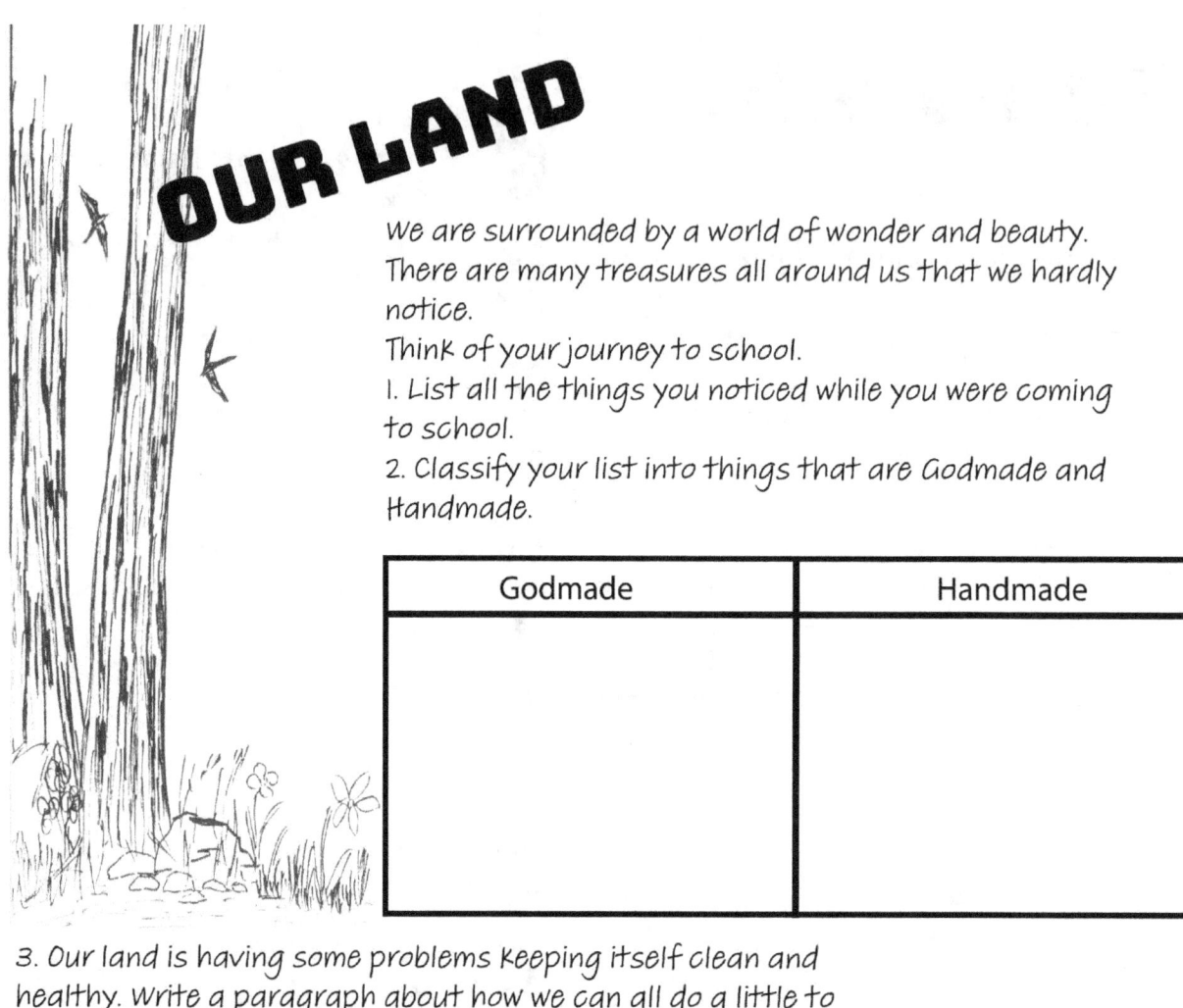

We are surrounded by a world of wonder and beauty. There are many treasures all around us that we hardly notice.

Think of your journey to school.

1. List all the things you noticed while you were coming to school.

2. Classify your list into things that are Godmade and Handmade.

Godmade	Handmade

3. Our land is having some problems keeping itself clean and healthy. Write a paragraph about how we can all do a little to make our planet what God wants it to be.

_____

_____

_____

_____

BAPTISM

Your baptism, and first Communion were special times in your life. Draw some of the special things that happened at these celebrations.

COMMUNION

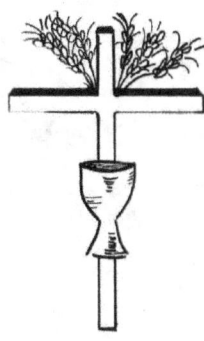

PRAY

LOVE

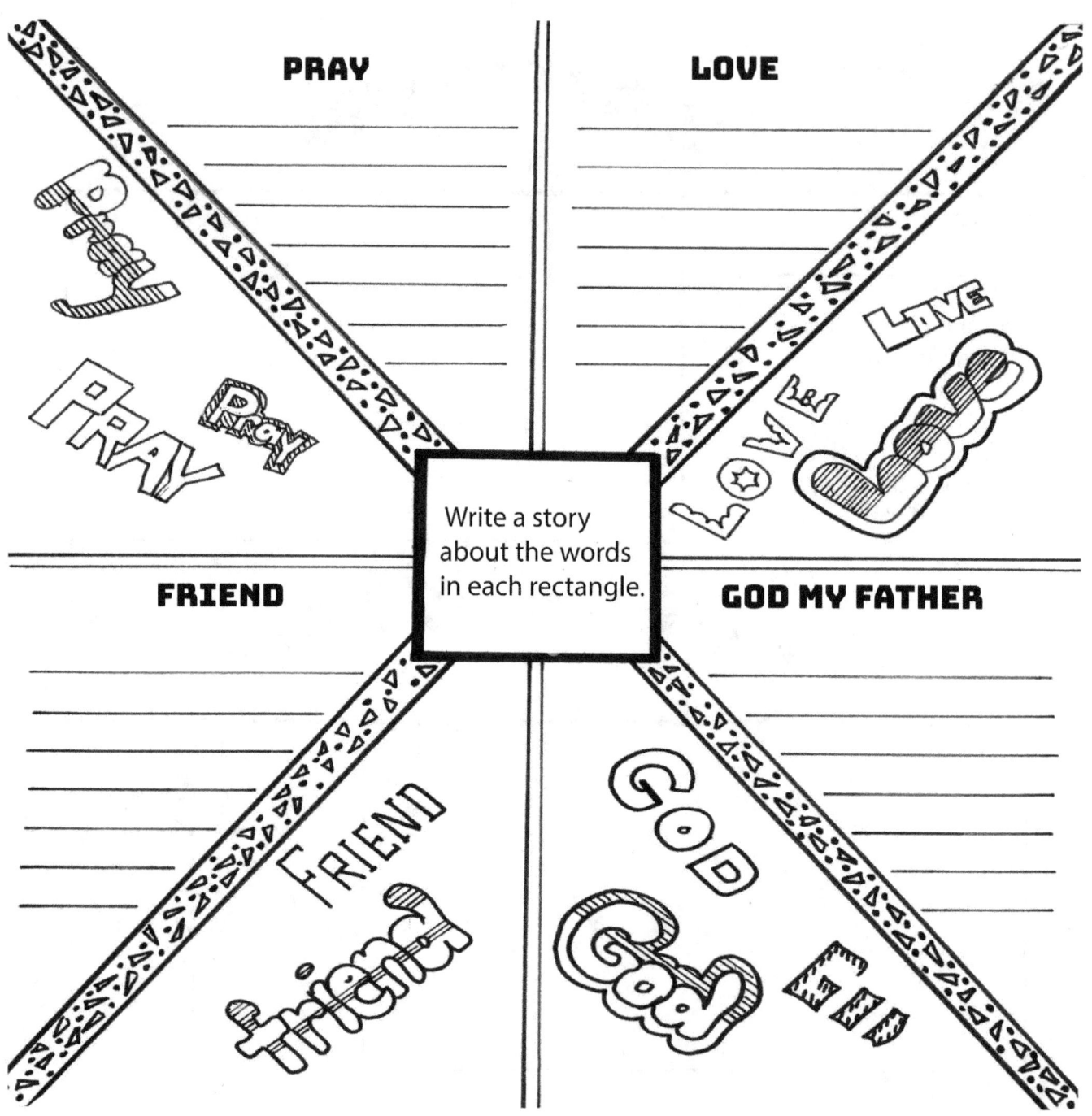

FRIEND

GOD MY FATHER

Write a story
about the words
in each rectangle.

In each letter of this word, write a special gift that you have. Cut out the word and display it.

Jesus calls you to be SPECIAL. He gave you special gifts that help you become special. Sometimes the gifts make you a good athelete, or artist, or writer, or _____.

What are your gifts?

PLAN A PLAY!

Get together with a friend.
Plan what you will say, what sounds you will
need, what you will wear, and where your play
will be.

Some ideas: Jesus goes on trial.
Mary sees Jesus carrying the cross.
Mary and John watch Jesus suffer.
Jesus rises up from the dead.

Decorate this message from Jesus to you.

I Love you because

YOU

are special

SPRING IS A TIME TO GROW

During Spring we see many new things come to life. We see new leaves on bushes and trees, new flowers spring up, new animals being born, and new food growing in the field. Because Spring is so special, let's celebrate it in a special way.
For every letter in the word SPRING, find words from nature (trees, flowers, animals, food) that begin with the same letter and write in the word.

Cut the word out, use your words in a spelling contest.

When we pray together we give Thanks to Jesus for all the wonderful gifts and blessings we have recieved.
We should also remember to thank all the people in our lives who help us to grow strong in Jesus' love.
Here are the names of some people who give us their love and care. Beside each name, tell how they help us grow..

My teacher(s) _____
_____
_____
_____

My parent(s) _____
_____
_____
_____

My friend(s) _____
_____
_____
_____

WE GROW

STRONG

IN PRAYER

READ ACTS 2: 1-41

Answer the questions

When does the Holy Spirit come into our lives?

_____
_____
_____
_____

What special gifts does the Spirit give us?

_____
_____
_____
_____

What does the Holy Spirit want us to do?

_____
_____
_____
_____

The dove is a symbol of the Holy Spirit.
Colour the dove, and inside of it write
the names of people who you would like
the Holy Spirit to help in a special way.

JESUS IS OUR LIGHT

This is a sunny note to your friend.
Tell your friend what gift you think God has given him or her.
Cut out the sunny note and give it to your friend.

Dear_____
You're my friend. I think that God had given you a special gift or talent. That gift is_____
_____
_____
_____
_____
_____
_____
_____
_____
_____
_____

Your friend,

_____

THE SPIRIT HELPS EVERYONE

At Pentecost the Holy Spirit called the Apostles to serve Jesus. The Holy Spirit gave them the power not to be afraid, and to trust in God. Today the Holy Spirit still calls people to serve the Lord.

who are some of the people in your life (friends, family, relatives) who have been called to serve Jesus?

Make a picture of people serving Jesus.

THANK YOU

Write a Thank you letter to the person you are most thankful for having in your life.

Dear _____

_____

_____

_____

_____

_____

_____

_____

_____

_____

_____

_____

_____

_____

_____

_____

_____

_____

_____

Thank you.

This planet was given to us for our use, not to abuse. We all must do our share to make it a WONDERFUL place to live.

Explain what the following people should do:

Me- _____
_____
_____

Principal- _____
_____
_____

Parents- _____
_____
_____

Government- _____
_____
_____

All life comes from God. We are asked to respect all life, and care for this planet.

TREASURES

What one person values may not be any value to another. It's important that we respect each other's treasures, even though we may not value them.

Draw treasures that belong to your Parents, Friend, Sister or Brother.

P
A
R
E
N
T
S

F
R
I
E
N
D

B   S
R   I
O R S
T   T
H   E
E   R
R

GOD'S SPIRIT GIVES US LIFE

READ: Mark 14:1-72- Jesus was arrested, left alone
by his friends, found guilty of a crime, and cruicified.

Answer these questions.

1. How did the Apostles feel?_____
_____
_____

2. What would you have done?_____
_____
_____

3. Have you ever felt alone and frightened?_____
_____
_____

4. What things frighten you?_____
_____
_____

Jesus thinks of everyone as a memeber of God's Family.
Jesus always made His friends feel welcome when they
visited him.

*Colour and decorate the word WELCOME.
*Cut it out and tape it to the Principal's door.
*Below, write down what you do to make your friends feel welcome.

_____
_____
_____
_____
_____
_____
_____
_____
_____
_____
_____
_____

Make a picture of all the Creatures that live in the sea.

FRIENDS come in all different shapes and sizes.

Read the following stories and tell who Jesus' friends are.

Matthew 4:18-22

Four of Jesus' friends were, _____

_____

Matthew 9:1-13

Jesus' new friend is _____

Make a picture of your friend. Tell us what they are doing.

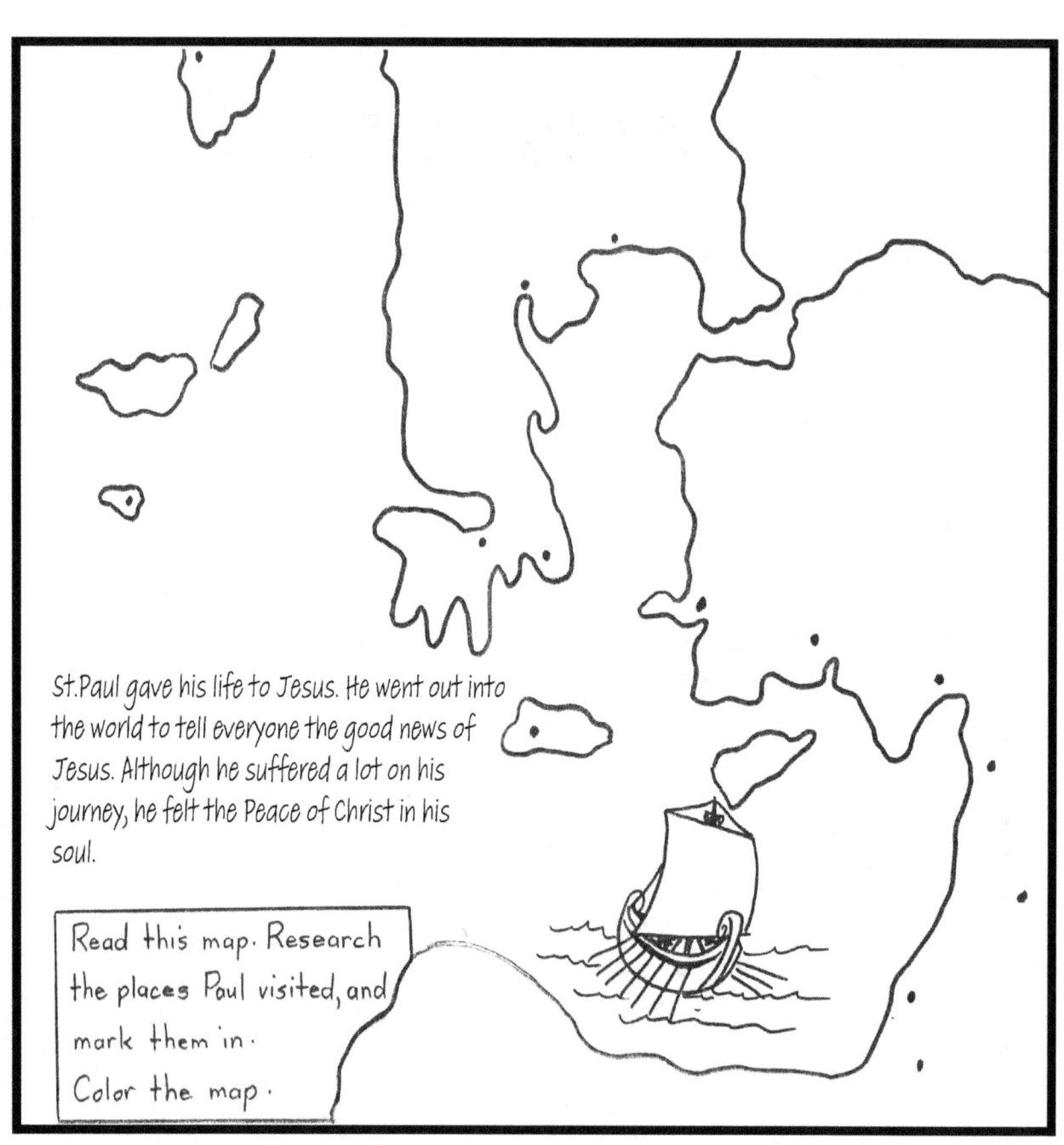

St.Paul gave his life to Jesus. He went out into the world to tell everyone the good news of Jesus. Although he suffered a lot on his journey, he felt the Peace of Christ in his soul.

Read this map. Research the places Paul visited, and mark them in. Color the map.

Pretend that it is Christmas and there is a family on your street that needs your help. You would like to raise money to buy them gifts.

Tell how you would raise the money, and draw the gift you would buy.

_____
_____
_____
_____
_____
_____

Parents	Tom (2 yrs)	John (8yrs)	Sue (12 yrs)

WE GIVE LIFE TO OTHERS

We are all influenced by the things around us. Sometimes we feel pressure from different things around us. That influence or pressure could be good or bad. Jesus felt pressure too. People around him wanted Jesus to be different.

Fill in the boxes below. Fill in names of those things that influenced Jesus. When you are finished make 2 sets of boxes for yourself and fill them in with good and bad pressures or influences.

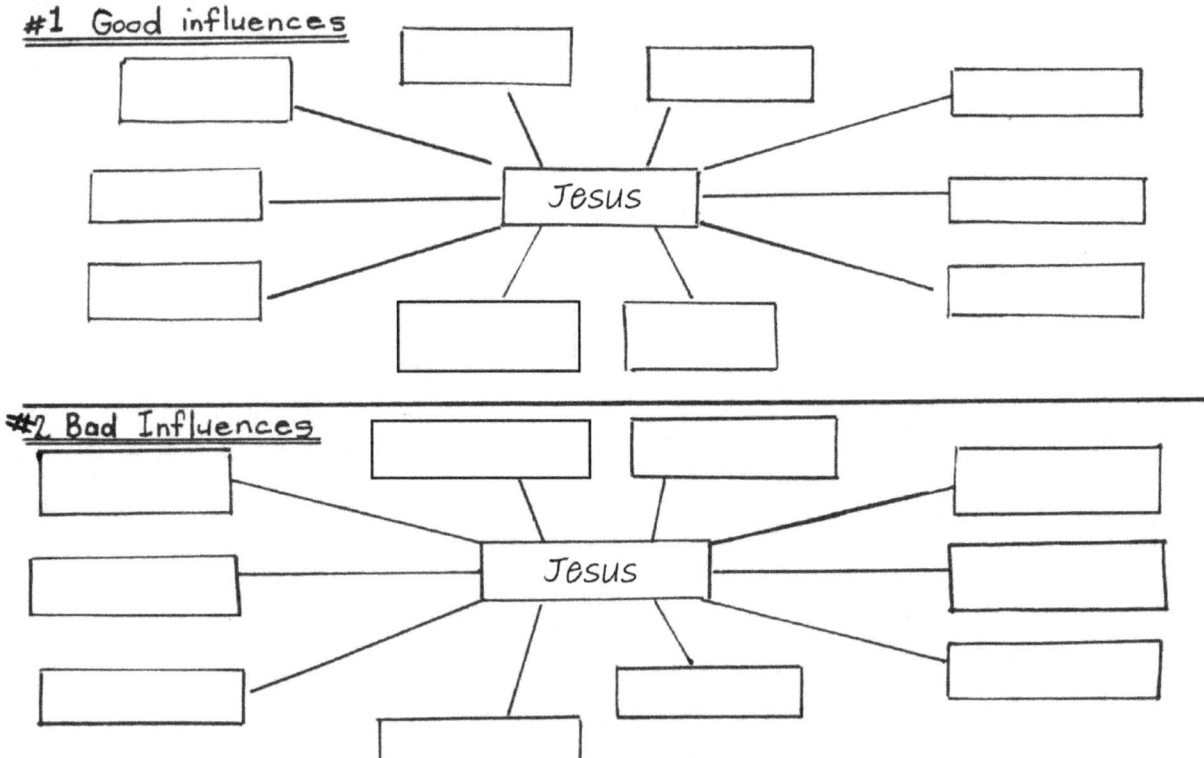

#1 Good influences

Jesus

#2 Bad Influences

Jesus

WORD SHAPES

Choose a symbol from Baptism or Communion.
Write a message around the shape.

A candle burns in church. It makes everything bright. candle candle

Find these words in this Puzzle.

D	D	A	E	R	B	P	C	L	E
G	O	D	P	A	R	E	N	T	S
O	O	C	F	W	Z	O	I	L	F
D	F	M	A	S	S	P	R	P	K
V	W	T	T	N	X	L	S	T	N
R	E	L	H	O	D	E	O	U	I
R	O	S	E	P	R	L	I	V	R
S	T	U	R	F	R	I	E	N	D

WATER   FRIENDS
OIL   ROSE
FATHER   GOD
MASS   PEOPLE
GODPARENTS
BREAD
FOOD
DRINK

Make your own wordsearch.
Use 10 words about God Our Father.
Give your puzzle to a friend.

Read Luke 9:10-17   Jesus always made people feel welcome.
Whenever people visited Jesus, he shared food with
them. The visitors enjoyed the food while they listened
to Jesus' teaching.

Below are some people sharing food with Jesus. What do you think they are
saying?

Paul persecuted the people who followed Jesus. Then Jesus healed Paul. After that Paul began spreading the world of Jesus around the world.

The FACES of ANGER

What was in Paul's heart before he met Jesus.

List the feelings...

_____
_____
_____
_____
_____
_____
_____

The FACES of PEACE

What was in Paul's heart after he met Jesus.

List the feelings...

_____
_____
_____
_____
_____
_____
_____

If you enjoyed this activity book you can find another one called:

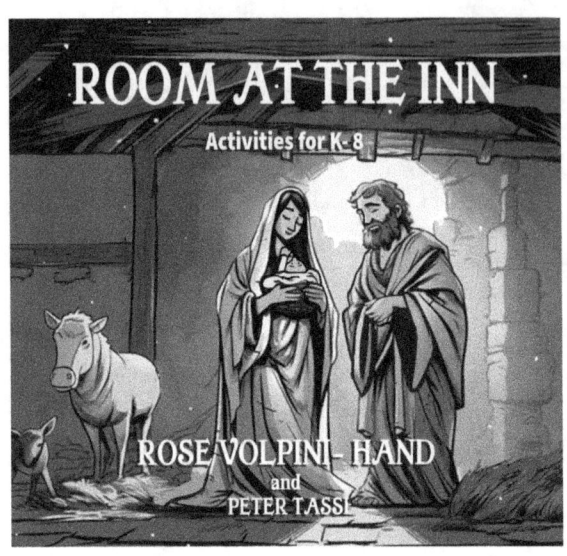